TABLE OF CONTENTS

T0042224

SECTION 1

AN INVISIBLE FORCE -------------- 4

SECTION 2

OPPOSITES ATTRACT ------------ 10

SECTION 3

MAGNETS IN SPACE ---------------16

SECTION 4

ELECTROMAGNETISM ----------- 22

More about Magnetism and Max Axiom........................28–29
Glossary 30
Read More 31
Internet Sites 31
Index... 32

A postcard from Japan gets Super Scientist Max Axiom thinking about the incredible power of magnetism.

Magnets are fascinating.

JAPAN

TUNNGK

They have the ability to attract some objects with an invisible force called magnetism.

Although we can't see this force, we use it every day.

But magnets do more than hold artwork and photos on the fridge.

GRAPHIC LIBRARY®

GRAPHIC SCIENCE

THE ATTRACTIVE STORY of

MAGNETISM

WITH MAX AXIOM

SUPER SCIENTIST

by Andrea Gianopoulos

illustrated by Cynthia Martin and Barbara Schulz

Consultant:

Leslie Flynn, PhD

Science Education

University of Minnesota

Capstone
PRESS

Mankato, Minnesota

Graphic Library is published by Capstone Press,
1710 Roe Crest Drive, North Mankato, MN 56003.
www.capstonepub.com

Library of Congress Cataloging-in-Publication Data
Gianopoulos, Andrea.
    The attractive story of magnetism with Max Axiom, super scientist / by Andrea
Gianopoulos; illustrated by Cynthia Martin and Barbara Schulz.
    p. cm.—(Graphic library. Graphic science)
    Summary: "In graphic novel format, follows the adventures of Max Axiom as he
explains the science behind magnetism"—Provided by publisher.
    Includes bibliographical references and index.
    ISBN-13: 978-1-4296-0141-2 (hardcover)   ISBN-10: 1-4296-0141-8 (hardcover)
    ISBN-13: 978-1-4296-1769-7 (softcover pbk.)   ISBN-10: 1-4296-1769-1 (softcover pbk.)
    1. Magnetism—Juvenile literature. 2. Magnets—Juvenile literature. 3. Adventure
stories—Juvenile literature. I. Martin, Cynthia, 1961- ill. II. Schulz, Barbara, ill.
III. Title. IV. Series.
QC753.7.G53 2008
538—dc22   2007002262

Art Director and Designer
Bob Lentz

Cover Artist
Tod Smith

Colorist
Krista Ward

Editor
Christopher L. Harbo

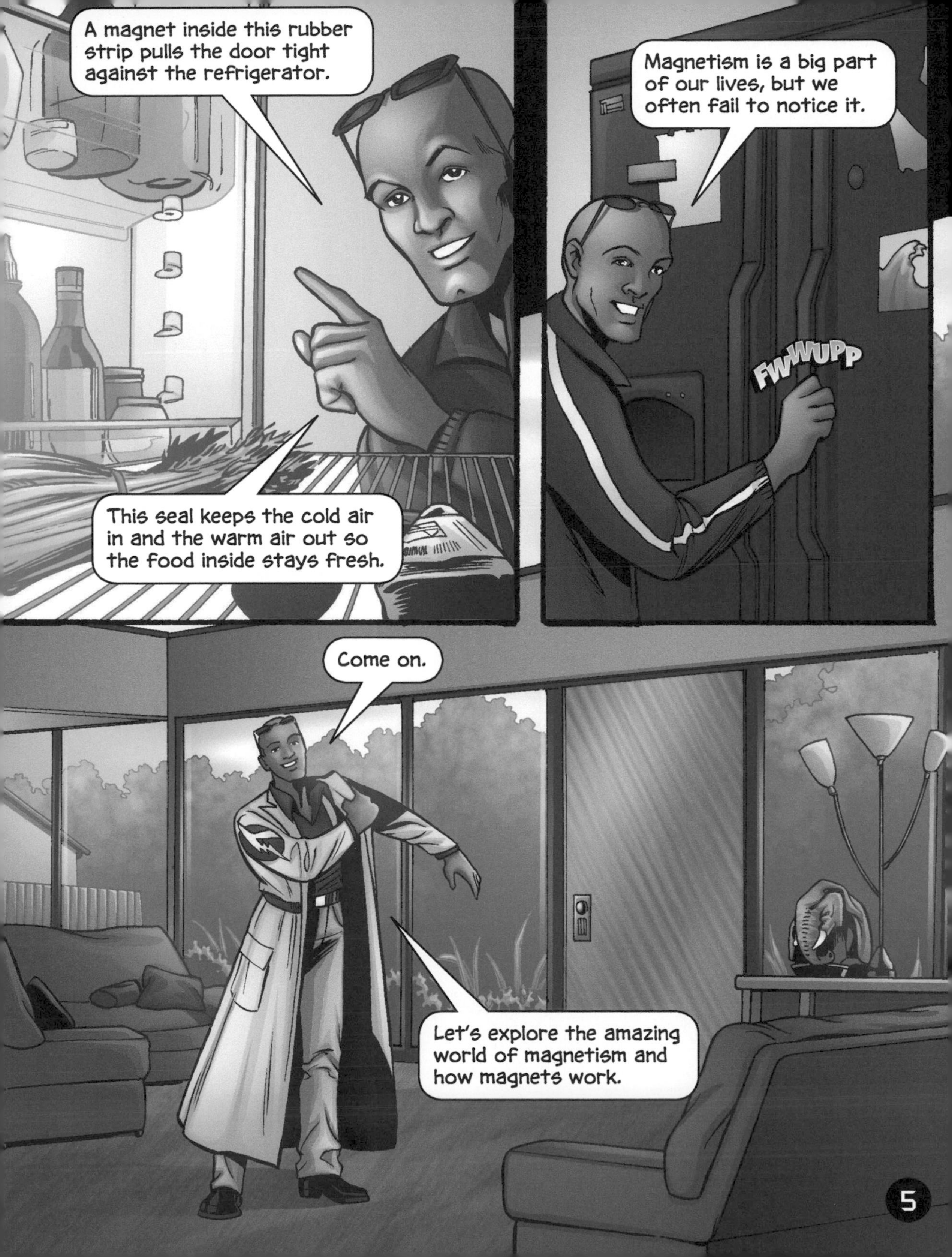
A magnet inside this rubber strip pulls the door tight against the refrigerator.
This seal keeps the cold air in and the warm air out so the food inside stays fresh.
Magnetism is a big part of our lives, but we often fail to notice it.
FWWUPP
Come on.
Let's explore the amazing world of magnetism and how magnets work.

Magnets have been around for thousands of years.

In fact, their history dates back to about 900 BC in ancient Greece's region of Magnesia.

Magnesian stone, now known as magnetite, littered Magnesia's countryside.

The word magnet comes from the Greek words "magnitis lithos," which mean "magnesian stone."

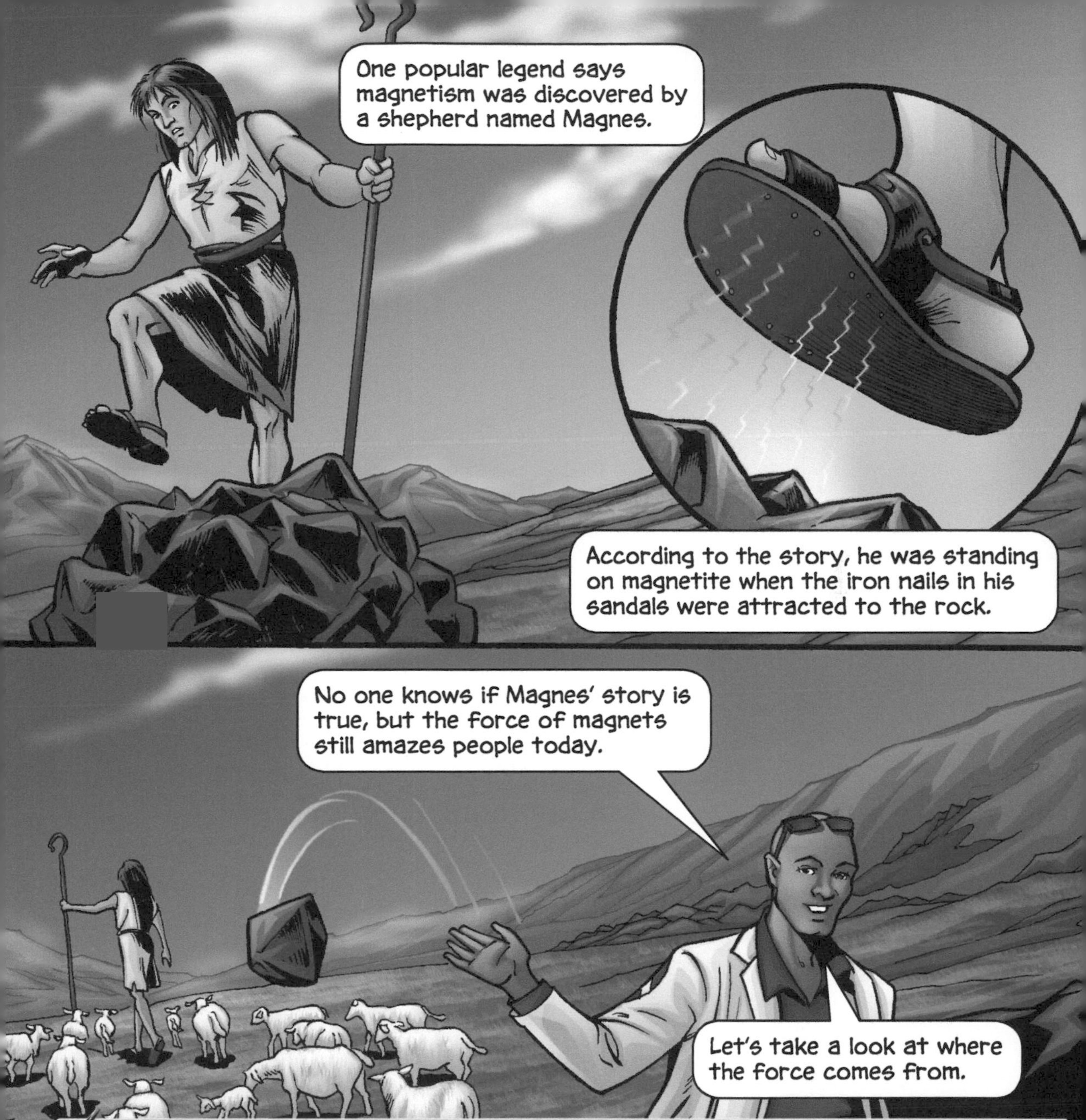
One popular legend says magnetism was discovered by a shepherd named Magnes.
According to the story, he was standing on magnetite when the iron nails in his sandals were attracted to the rock.
No one knows if Magnes' story is true, but the force of magnets still amazes people today.
Let's take a look at where the force comes from.

MAGNETIC MATERIALS

ACCESS GRANTED: MAX AXIOM

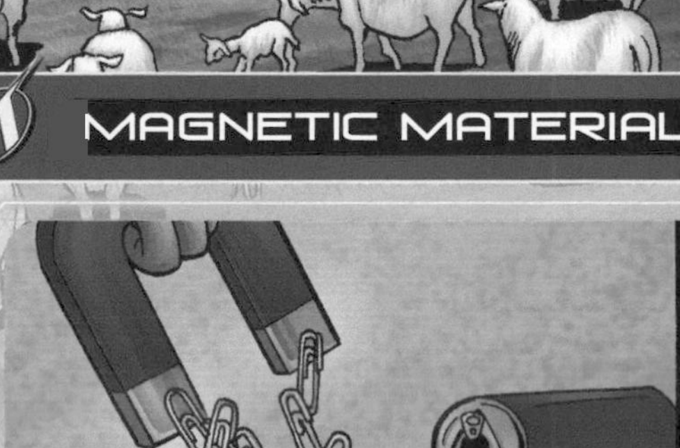

Magnetism attracts some metals, but not others. A magnet will easily pick up iron, steel, nickel, and cobalt. But it has no power over aluminum, copper, or gold.

To understand magnetism, you must first understand atoms.

Atoms are tiny particles too small to see with your eyes. They make up everything in the universe.

Every atom holds a nucleus surrounded by a cloud of electrons.

NUCLEUS

ELECTRON CLOUD

ELECTRON

The atoms in most materials have electrons that spin in different directions as they move around the nucleus.

In a magnet, the electrons spin in the same direction.

By spinning in the same direction, the electrons create a force.

This force is magnetism.

Magnets pass their magnetic power to the objects they attract. A steel washer stuck to a magnet becomes a temporary magnet itself. In fact, a chain of washers can dangle from the magnet as the magnetic force is passed from one washer to the next.

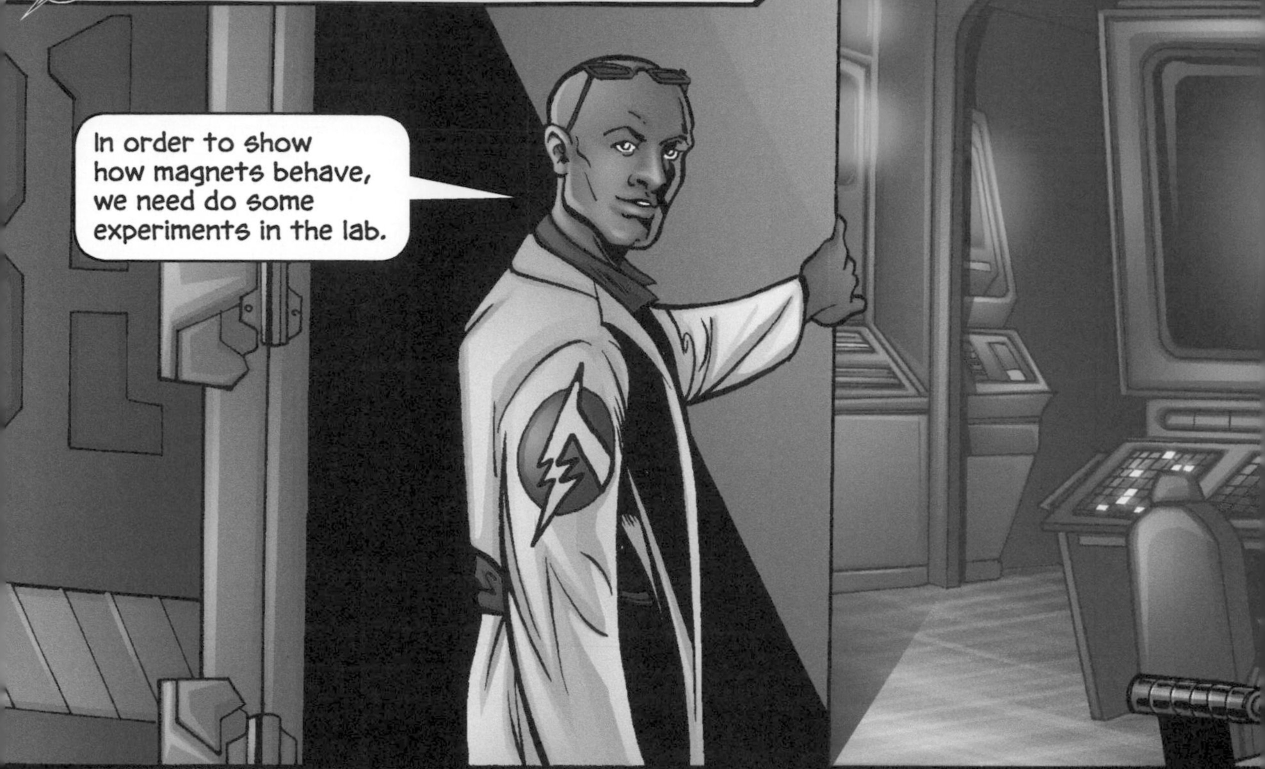
In order to show how magnets behave, we need do some experiments in the lab.

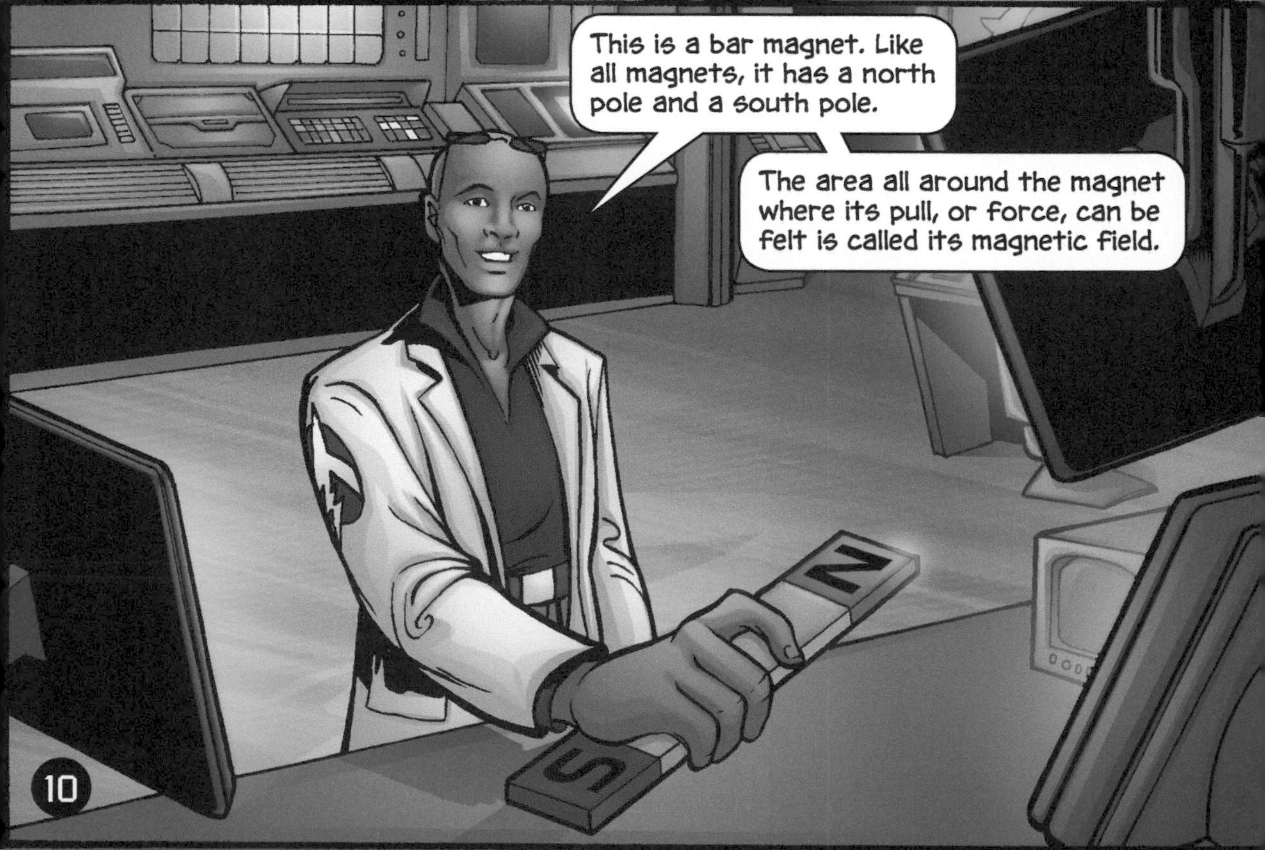
This is a bar magnet. Like all magnets, it has a north pole and a south pole.
The area all around the magnet where its pull, or force, can be felt is called its magnetic field.
N
S

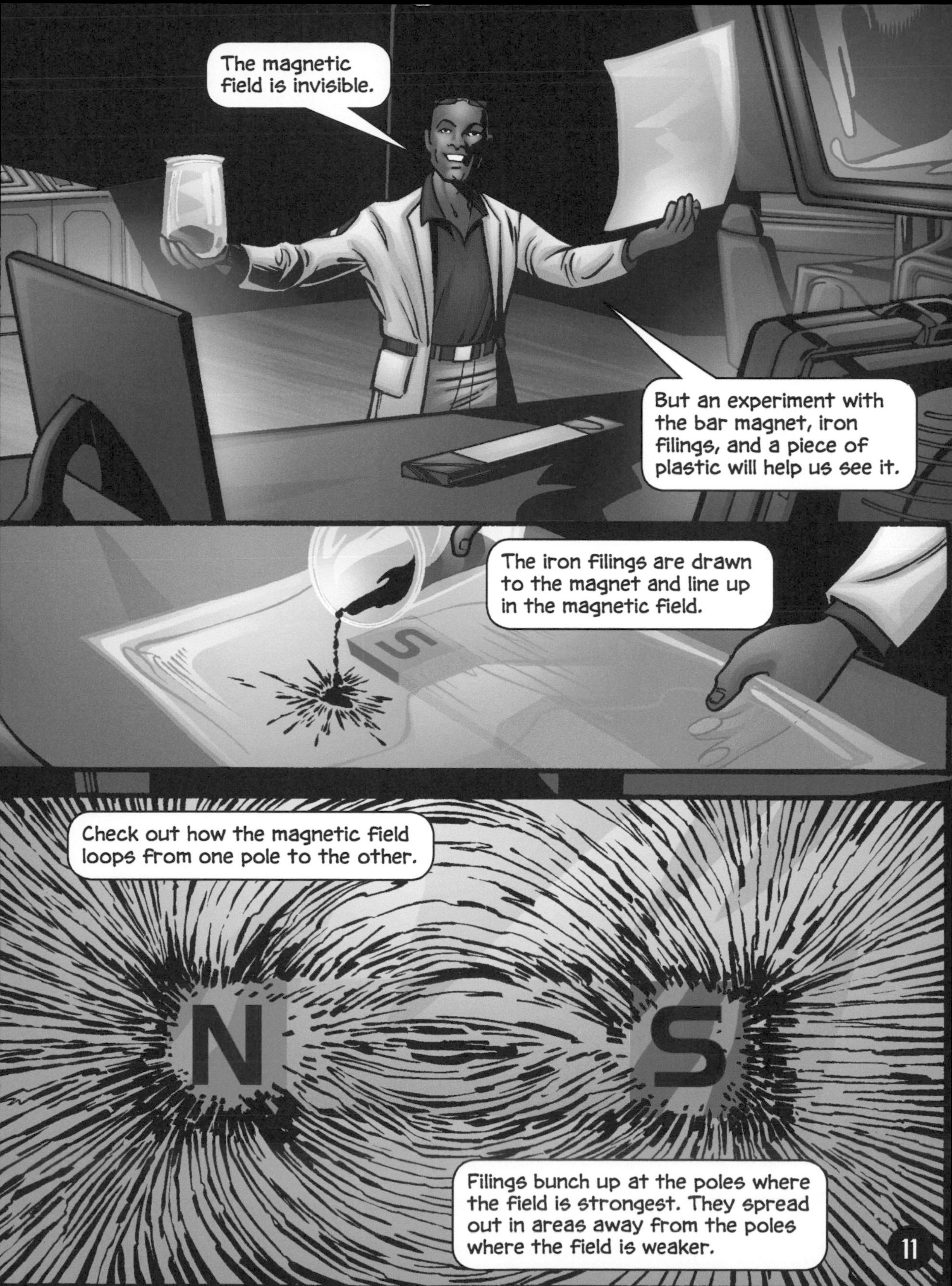
The magnetic field is invisible.
But an experiment with the bar magnet, iron filings, and a piece of plastic will help us see it.
S
The iron filings are drawn to the magnet and line up in the magnetic field.
Check out how the magnetic field loops from one pole to the other.
N
S
Filings bunch up at the poles where the field is strongest. They spread out in areas away from the poles where the field is weaker.

The magnetic field of one magnet can provide hours of entertainment.

But check out what happens when two magnets come together.

When I bring two magnets together, I can feel the push or pull of their magnetic fields.

N S

SNAP!

What makes magnets push apart or pull together?

The answer lies in their poles. Like poles repel and opposite poles attract.

S N S N

When I bring the north poles of both magnets together, their magnetic fields push away from each other.

No matter how hard I try, two like poles won't join together.

When I bring a south pole and a north pole together, they pull toward each other.

They are attracted because their magnetic fields line up.

SNNAPP!

Now, the magnetic field loops from one magnet's south pole to the other's north pole.

Two small magnets become one larger, stronger magnet.

13

The way these bar magnets join together is a good example of what happens millions of times inside a magnet.

Let's take a look at what I mean.

Magnets are made of millions of micromagnets called domains. Each domain is packed with atoms whose electrons spin in the same direction.

DOMAINS

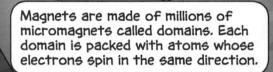

The more domains that line up in a magnet, the stronger the magnetic field becomes.

While a magnet's domains line up, the domains in other objects aren't well organized.

For instance, the domains in this steel paper clip point in many directions.

Because magnets attract steel, a magnet can affect the direction a paper clip's domains point.

By rubbing a magnet over the paper clip in one direction, the domains inside the paper clip line up.

The paper clip becomes a magnet itself. It can attract other paper clips.

Most magnets are small enough to fit in our hands, but some magnets are huge.

I know a scientist in the Canadian Arctic who can tell us how our own planet acts like a giant magnet.

Hello, Max. What science topic are you studying this time?

Magnets, Dr. Mink. I need information about earth's magnetic power.

Earth's magnetism comes from deep beneath its surface. In the planet's outer core, hot magma made of iron and nickel slowly rises and falls.

OUTER CORE

The moving magma creates electrical currents that form a magnetic field.

That means earth has north and south magnetic poles just like this bar magnet.

That's right, Max. Earth's magnetic poles are located close to the geographic North and South Poles.

MAGNETIC NORTH POLE

GEOGRAPHIC NORTH POLE

But earth's magnetic field moves. This movement causes the magnetic poles to shift about 25 miles, or 40 kilometers, each year.

In fact, I'm looking for the current location of the magnetic north pole here in the Canadian Arctic.

Good luck! And thanks for the information, Dr. Mink.

⚡ TWISTING FIELD

Earth's magnetic field twists and wobbles. Sometimes, it even reverses. About every 300,000 years, earth's north magnetic pole becomes the south magnetic pole.

On a daily basis, we don't usually notice earth's magnetic field.

But we can see its effects if we know where to look.

Next stop—outer space!

SHHHSSSOOO!!!

The sun gives us light, but it also bombards our planet with lots of particles like electrons. These particles form what scientists call the solar wind.

MAGNETOSPHERE

EARTH

The solar wind blows across earth's magnetic field, or magnetosphere, making it lopsided.

Sometimes the sun shoots off billions of particles in an explosion called a solar flare.

SOLAR FLARE

The particles flood earth's magnetosphere.

VAN ALLEN BELTS

They bounce back and forth between the north and south magnetic poles in an area called the Van Allen Belts.

So many particles flood the magnetic field that some of them begin spiraling down toward earth at the magnetic poles.

The particles collide with gases in earth's atmosphere, causing them to glow.

These curtains of color are called the Aurora Borealis or northern lights and the Aurora Australis or southern lights.

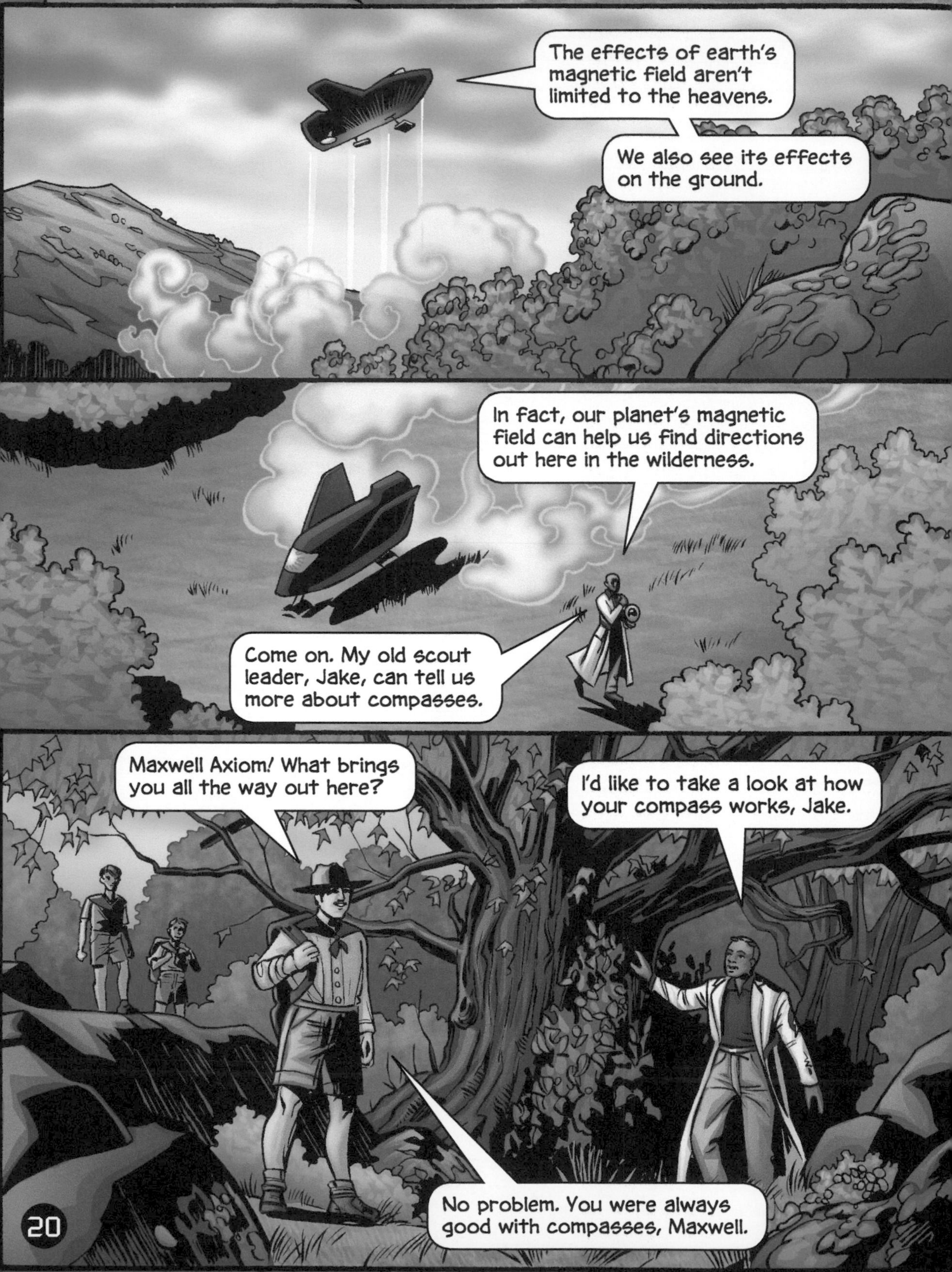

The effects of earth's magnetic field aren't limited to the heavens.
We also see its effects on the ground.
In fact, our planet's magnetic field can help us find directions out here in the wilderness.
Come on. My old scout leader, Jake, can tell us more about compasses.
Maxwell Axiom! What brings you all the way out here?
I'd like to take a look at how your compass works, Jake.
No problem. You were always good with compasses, Maxwell.

Like most compasses, yours has a needle that spins on a pivot.

That's right. The needle is a small bar magnet. As it spins, its points are drawn toward earth's magnetic poles.

NEEDLE

PIVOT

The red end always points north and the grey end always points south.

Correct. And once we know the direction of north and south, we can figure out the direction of east and west.

Sounds like a compass is a great tool to have on a hike. Thanks, Jake!

Any time, Maxwell.

FINDING EAST

Finding north and south on a compass is easy. But what about east or west? Finding these directions is easier than you think. To find east, hold the compass level and rotate it so the letter E is on top. Now, slowly turn your body until the red tip of the needle points to the letter N. When it does, you are facing east.

The compass needles, bar magnets, and refrigerator magnets we've seen all have something in common.

They're all permanent magnets. Their magnetic power never stops working.

But not all magnets have their power all of the time.

Electromagnets get their power from electricity and their magnetism is temporary.

Electromagnets sound complicated, but they're really quite simple.

When electricity flows through a wire, it creates a magnetic field. In a straight wire, that magnetic field is weak.

But if the wire is coiled around an iron bar, the field becomes much stronger.

MAGNETIC FIELD

MAGNETIC FIELD

Electromagnets, like the one on this crane, are very useful because they can be turned on and off.

CCRRRAASSHH!

Powered up, the magnet can lift a car off the ground with ease.

Then, with the flip of a switch, it can release the car from its grip.

Electromagnets are good for more than just picking up junked cars.

Scientists and engineers are testing the power of electromagnets on trains.

Magnetic levitation, or maglev, trains don't have wheels.

Instead, electromagnets under the train's carriage and in a guideway repel each other.

The repelling magnets make the train hover above and move along the bottom of the guideway.

Maglev trains can travel more than 300 miles or 483 kilometers per hour.

WWHHHHOOOOOOSSHH

Without engines, they don't create a lot of noise or air pollution.

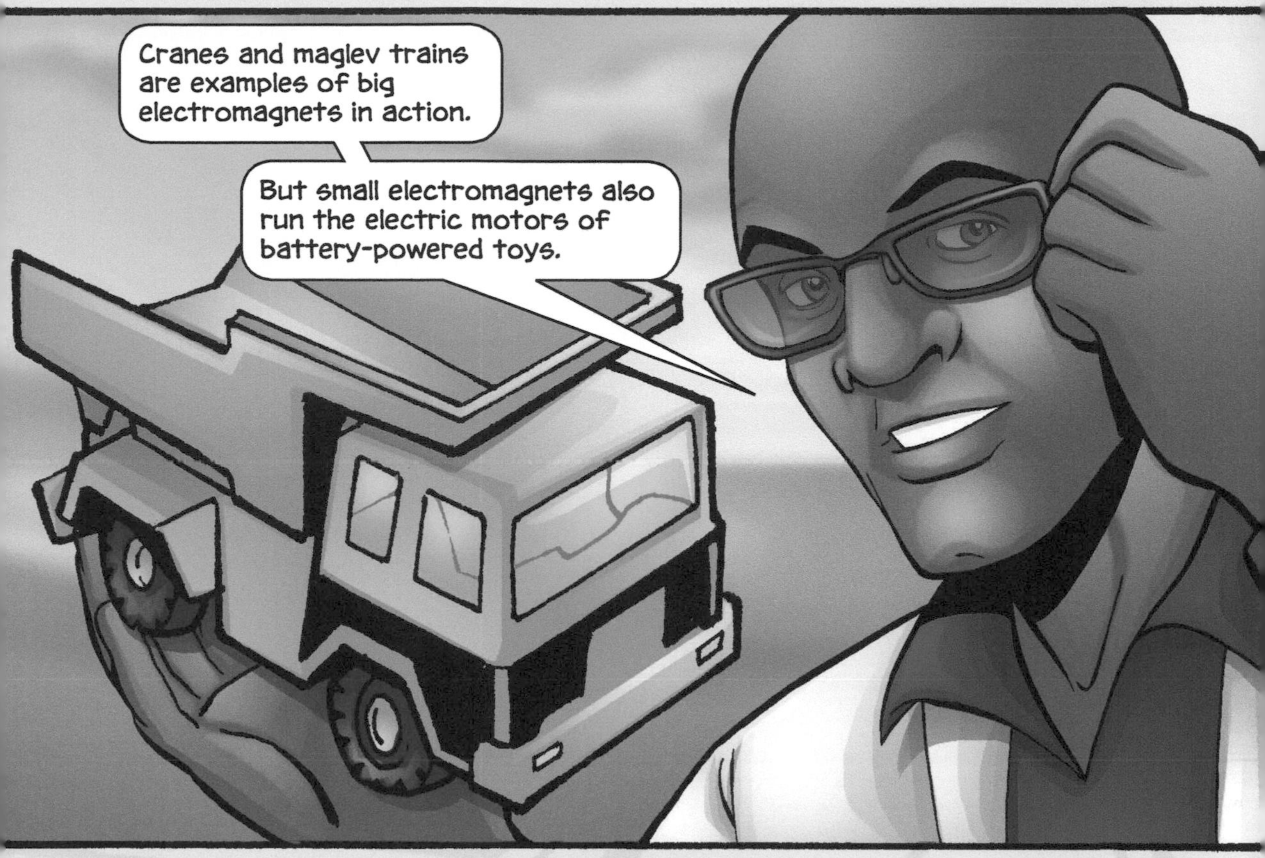
Cranes and maglev trains are examples of big electromagnets in action.
But small electromagnets also run the electric motors of battery-powered toys.

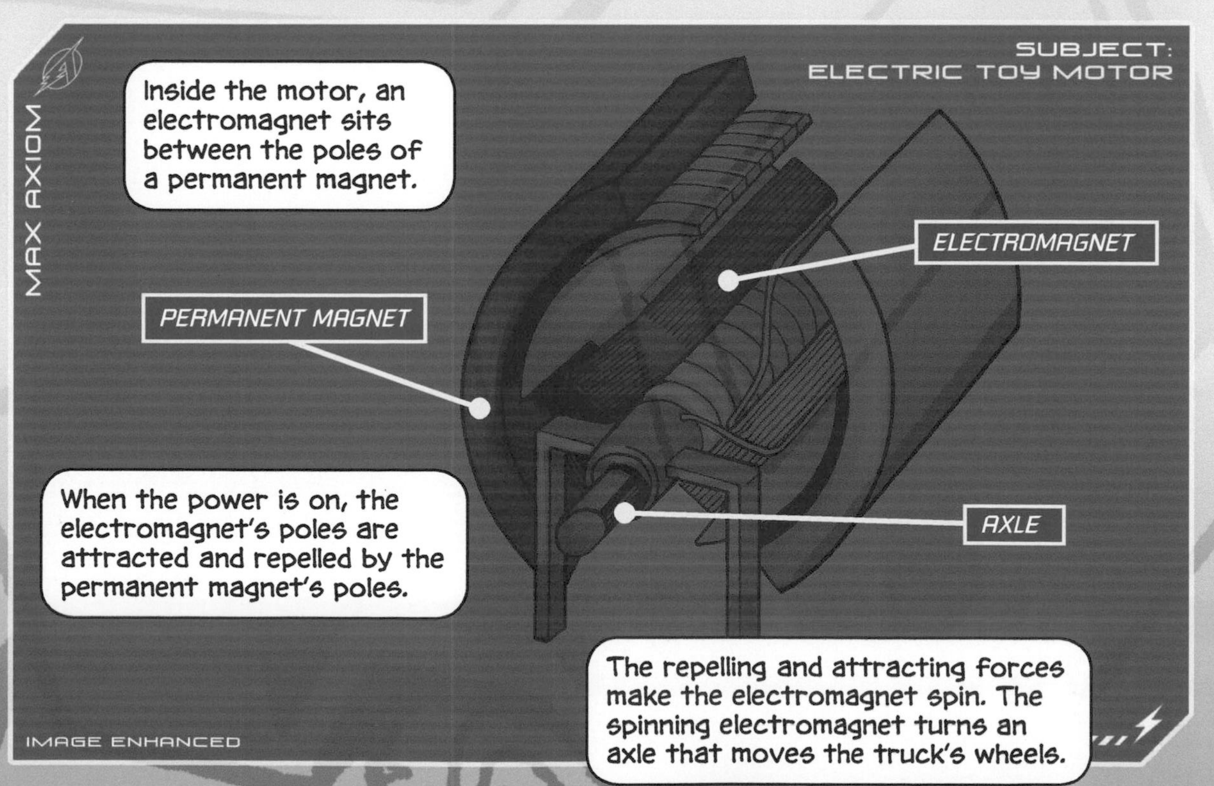
MAX AXIOM
SUBJECT:
ELECTRIC TOY MOTOR
Inside the motor, an electromagnet sits between the poles of a permanent magnet.
ELECTROMAGNET
PERMANENT MAGNET
AXLE
When the power is on, the electromagnet's poles are attracted and repelled by the permanent magnet's poles.
The repelling and attracting forces make the electromagnet spin. The spinning electromagnet turns an axle that moves the truck's wheels.
IMAGE ENHANCED

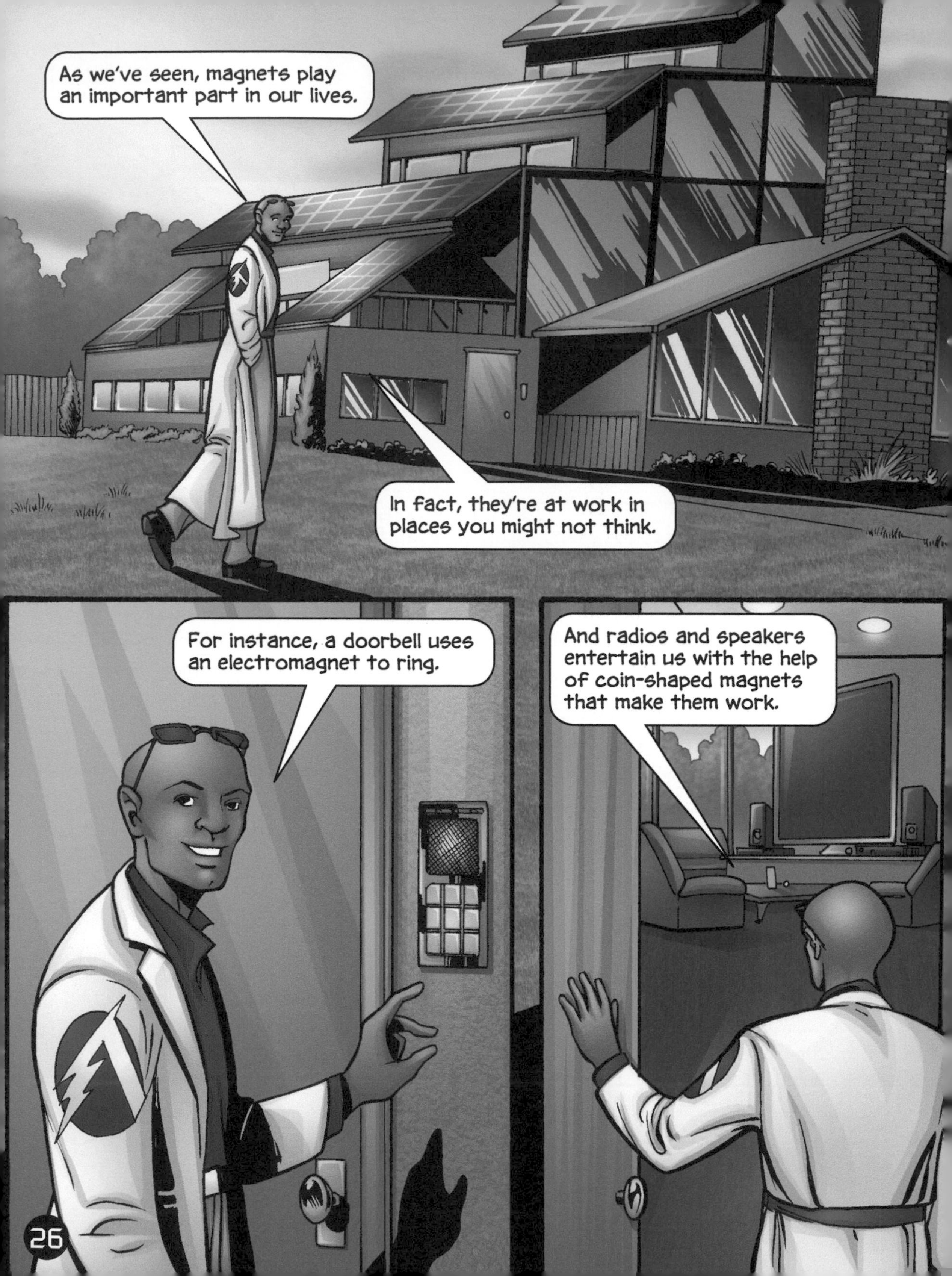
As we've seen, magnets play an important part in our lives.
In fact, they're at work in places you might not think.
For instance, a doorbell uses an electromagnet to ring.
And radios and speakers entertain us with the help of coin-shaped magnets that make them work.

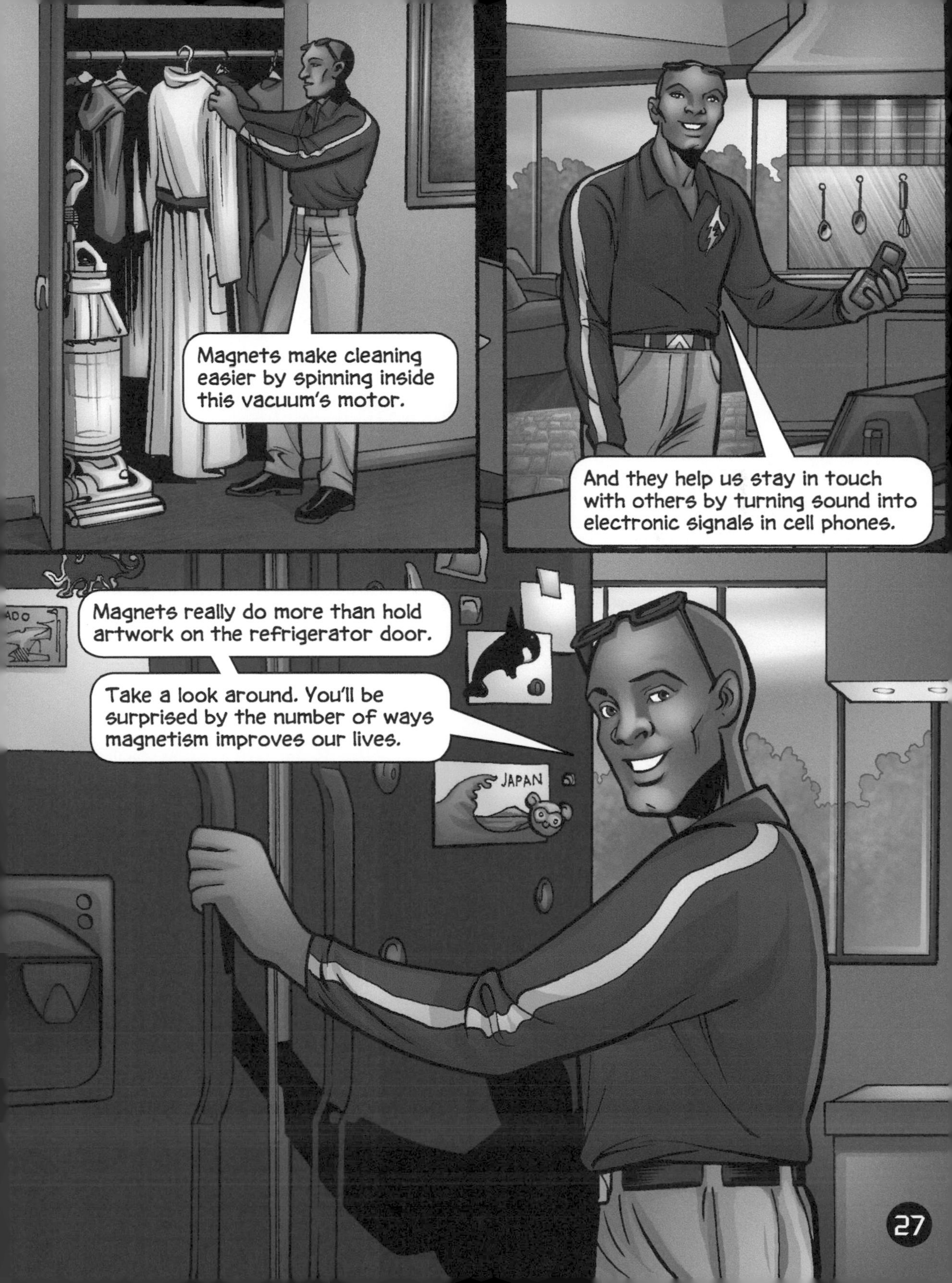
Magnets make cleaning easier by spinning inside this vacuum's motor.
And they help us stay in touch with others by turning sound into electronic signals in cell phones.
Magnets really do more than hold artwork on the refrigerator door.
Take a look around. You'll be surprised by the number of ways magnetism improves our lives.
JAPAN

MORE ABOUT MAGNETISM

Some animals sense earth's magnetic field and use it to help them find their way. Whales, dolphins, and many birds use earth's magnetic field during migration. Australia's compass termites always build their nests facing north.

Earth's north magnetic pole has moved about 700 miles (1,127 kilometers) since it was first discovered in 1831. If it continues moving at its current speed and direction, the north magnetic pole will be located in Siberia by 2050.

Some farmers make their cattle swallow a magnet to keep them healthy. This small magnet attracts nails and pieces of wire they accidentally eat while grazing. The magnet keeps the bits of metal from passing through their stomachs and damaging their other organs.

The National High Magnetic Field Laboratory at Florida State University in Tallahassee has the world's largest magnet. This giant magnet stands 16 feet (5 meters) tall and weighs more than 30,000 pounds (13,608 kilograms). Scientists developed the magnet for 13 years at a cost of $16.5 million.

The sun has a very strong magnetic field. Over time, this field gets knotted and twisted creating dark-colored sunspots on the sun's surface. Sunspots always come in pairs. One is a north magnetic pole while the other is a south magnetic pole.

The sun's magnetic field flips every 11 years. The north magnetic pole becomes a south magnetic pole and the south magnetic pole becomes a north magnetic pole.

Can a magnet attract a penny? Not a United States penny. U.S. pennies are made mostly of zinc and copper. Neither zinc nor copper is magnetic. British pennies are another story. They are made mostly of steel coated with a thin layer of copper. A magnet will easily pick up British pennies because magnets attract steel.

MORE ABOUT

SUPER SCIENTIST

Real name: Maxwell J. Axiom
Hometown: Seattle, Washington
Height: 6' 1"   **Weight:** 192 lbs
Eyes: Brown   **Hair:** None

Super capabilities: Super intelligence; able to shrink to the size of an atom; sunglasses give x-ray vision; lab coat allows for travel through time and space.

Origin: Since birth, Max Axiom seemed destined for greatness. His mother, a marine biologist, taught her son about the mysteries of the sea. His father, a nuclear physicist and volunteer park ranger, schooled Max on the wonders of earth and sky.

One day on a wilderness hike, a megacharged lightning bolt struck Max with blinding fury. When he awoke, Max discovered a newfound energy and set out to learn as much about science as possible. He traveled the globe earning degrees in every aspect of the field. Upon his return, he was ready to share his knowledge and new identity with the world. He had become Max Axiom, Super Scientist.

GLOSSARY

atom (AT-uhm)—an element in its smallest form

domain (doh-MAYN)—a group of magnetic atoms

electromagnet (e-lek-troh-MAG-nit)—a temporary magnet created when an electric current flows through a conductor

electron (e-LEK-tron)—a tiny particle in an atom that travels around the nucleus

magma (MAG-muh)—melted rock found beneath the surface of earth

magnetic field (mag-NET-ik FEELD)—the area around a magnet that has the power to attract magnetic metals

magnetite (MAG-nuh-tite)—a hard, black rock found in earth that attracts iron; magnetite is also known as lodestone.

magnetosphere (mag-NET-ohs-sfir)—the magnetic field extending into space around a planet or star

nucleus (NOO-klee-uhss)—the center of an atom; a nucleus is made up of neutrons and protons.

pivot (PIV-uht)—a point on which something turns or balances

pole (POHL)—one of the two ends of a magnet; a pole can also be the top or bottom part of a planet.

repel (ri-PEL)—to push apart; like poles of magnets repel each other.

temporary (TEM-puh-rer-ee)—lasting only a short time

READ MORE

Cooper, Christopher. *Magnetism: From Pole to Pole.* Science Answers. Chicago: Heinemann Library, 2004.

Morgan, Ben. *Magnetism.* Elementary Physics. San Diego: Blackbirch Press, 2003.

Nelson, Robin. *Magnets.* First Step Nonfiction. Minneapolis: Lerner, 2004.

Parker, Steve. *Opposites Attract: Magnetism.* Everyday Science. Chicago. Heinemann Library, 2005.

Richardson, Adele. *Magnetism: A Question and Answer Book.* Questions and Answers: Physical Science. Mankato, Minn.: Capstone Press, 2006.

INTERNET SITES

FactHound offers a safe, fun way to find Internet sites related to this book. All of the sites on FactHound have been researched by our staff.

Here's how:
1. Visit *www.facthound.com*
2. Choose your grade level.
3. Type in this book ID **1429601418** for age-appropriate sites. You may also browse subjects by clicking on letters, or by clicking on pictures and words.
4. Click on the **Fetch It** button.

FactHound will fetch the best sites for you!

INDEX

animals, 28
atoms, 8–9, 14
attracting forces, 4, 5, 7, 9, 10, 11, 12–13, 15, 21, 25, 28, 29
Aurora Australis, 19
Aurora Borealis, 19

bar magnets, 10, 11, 12–13, 14, 17, 21, 22

compasses, 20–21, 22
cow magnets, 28

domains, 14–15

earth, 16–17, 18, 19, 20, 21, 28
electric motors, 25, 27
electromagnets, 22–25, 26
electrons, 8–9, 14, 18

maglev trains, 24, 25
Magnes, 7
Magnesia, 6
magnetic fields, 10–13, 14, 16, 17, 18, 19, 20, 23, 28, 29
magnetic poles, 10, 11, 12–13, 17, 19, 21, 25, 28, 29
magnetite, 6–7
magnetosphere, 18, 19
magnets
  creation of, 15, 16, 23
  uses of, 4–5, 20–21, 23–25, 26–27, 28

metals
  cobalt, 7
  iron, 7, 11, 16, 23
  nickel, 7, 16
  steel, 7, 9, 15, 29

northern lights. *See* Aurora Borealis

paper clips, 15
pennies, 29
permanent magnets, 22, 25

refrigerator magnets, 4, 22, 27
repelling forces, 12–13, 24, 25

solar flares, 19
solar wind, 18
southern lights. *See* Aurora Australis
sun, 18–19, 28, 29
sunspots, 28

temporary magnets, 9, 22

Van Allen Belts, 19